THE MAGNIFICENT BOOK OF FANTASY CREATURES

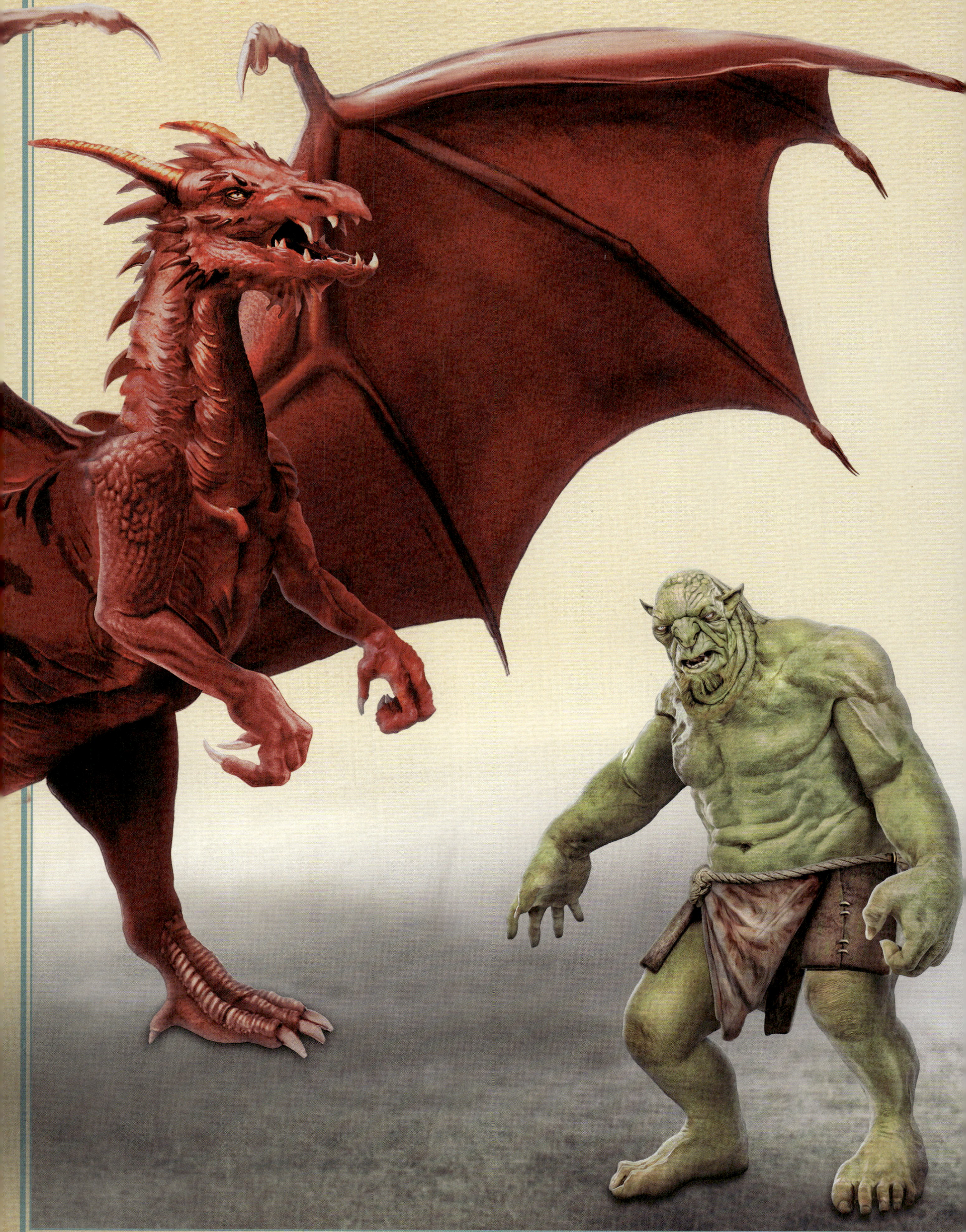

THE MAGNIFICENT BOOK OF FANTASY CREATURES

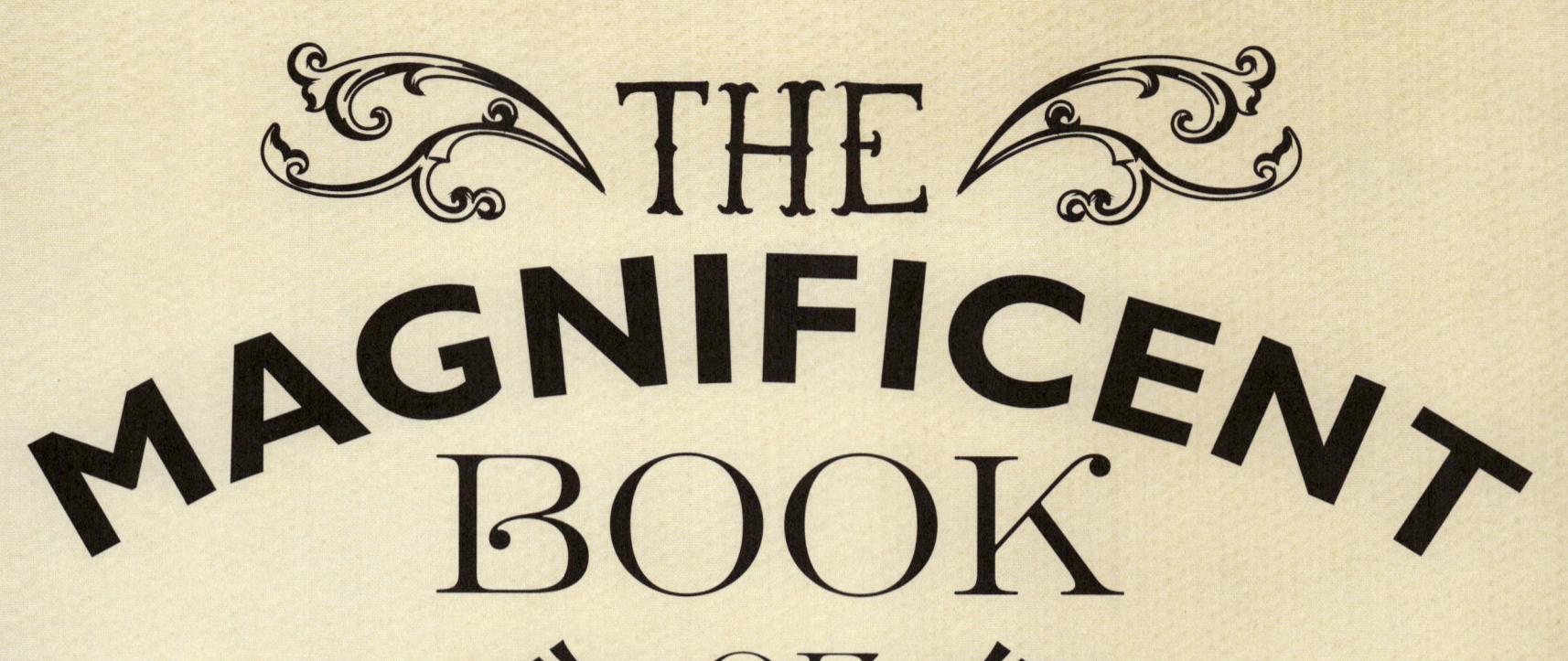

ILLUSTRATED BY
Val Walerczuk

WRITTEN BY
Tom Jackson

WeldonOwen
PUBLISHING

WeldonOwen
PUBLISHING

First published in the UK by
Weldon Owen
King's Road Publishing
The Plaza
535 King's Road
London SW10 0SZ
www.weldonowen.co.uk
www.bonnierpublishing.com

Author: Tom Jackson
Illustrator: Val Walerczuk
Senior Editor: Lydia Halliday
Designer: Anna Pond
Publisher: Donna Gregory

Copyright © 2017 Weldon Owen

All rights reserved. No part of this publication may be reproduced, stored in a retrieval system or transmitted in any form or by any means, electronic, mechanical, photocopying, recording, or otherwise, without the prior written permission of the copyright holder and the publisher.

Printed in China

10 9 8 7 6 5 4 3 2 1

ISBN: 978-1-78342-333-0

Introduction

Let's take a look at some magnificent fantasy creatures. You may recognize many of the animals in this book, such as mermaids, dragons, and unicorns, but others will look very strange and unreal. For example, the basilisk is a snake with a chicken's head, while Ammit is a monster with a crocodile's head, a lion's mane, and a hippo's bottom! For many centuries, people believed that these creatures were as real as lions, horses, and snakes. The beasts were even included in early biology books with advice on where to find them and how to protect yourself from their terrifying attacks. However, all of these fantastic animals are completely made up; they are not real and never have been. Instead, they appear in famous stories and legends about monsters, heroes, and magic. Some of them are helpful creatures. For example, the lóng, or Chinese dragon, watches over the land and provides water for crops, and the thunderbirds of North America fight off evil spirits that cause catastrophic storms. Other creatures are pure evil: Scottish water spirits, or kelpies, lure people into dangerous rivers, while trolls raided Viking homes to steal food and kidnap people. Together, the fantasy creatures tell some incredible stories. Read on to find out more. Have a magnificent time!

Legend

Theories on catching a unicorn

Unicorns have traditionally been presented as being almost impossible to catch. Cosmas Indicopleustes, a Christian Egyptian of the sixth century CE, travelled in Africa and to India and reported about the strange creatures that he saw. He said that unicorns were always able to escape thanks to their strong horn. The unicorn would simply jump off a cliff to get away, it then turned in the air so that it landed on its horn, which would protect it from the fall.

Contents

Dragon	8	Unicorn	26
Gorgon	10	Elf	28
Kraken	12	Phoenix	30
Giant	14	Bunyip	32
Kelpie	16	Jinni	34
Fairy	18	Basilisk	36
Ammit	20	Gnome	38
Harpy	22	Mannegishi	40
Ogre	24	Banshee	42

Griffin	44	Yeti	62
Troll	46	Lóng Dragon	64
Jorogumo	48	Cyclops	66
Thunderbird	50	Amphisbaena	68
Mermaid	52	Vampire	70
Minotaur	54	Hydra	72
Cerberus	56	Centaur	74
Ghoul	58	Leviathan	76
Chimera	60	Sphynx	78

Dragon

- The Old-English poem *Beowulf*, tells the story of a great monster-slaying hero who killed a fire-breathing dragon that was guarding a treasure-hoard of gold. However, Beowulf himself was killed in the process.

- According to an eastern European tradition, a giant dragon called Bolla sleeps all year and only wakes up for a day each spring to eat one person before going back to sleep again.

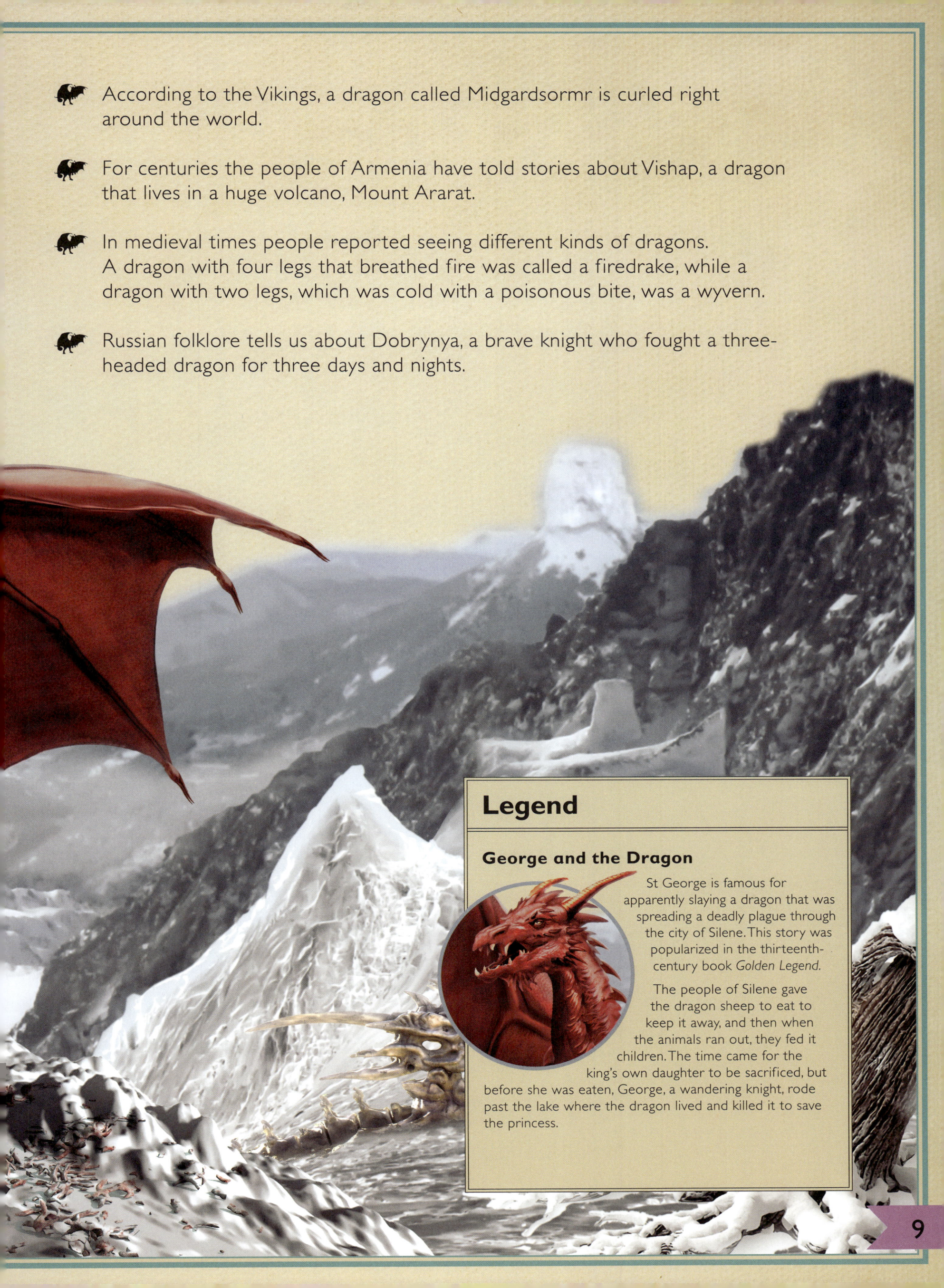

- According to the Vikings, a dragon called Midgardsormr is curled right around the world.

- For centuries the people of Armenia have told stories about Vishap, a dragon that lives in a huge volcano, Mount Ararat.

- In medieval times people reported seeing different kinds of dragons. A dragon with four legs that breathed fire was called a firedrake, while a dragon with two legs, which was cold with a poisonous bite, was a wyvern.

- Russian folklore tells us about Dobrynya, a brave knight who fought a three-headed dragon for three days and nights.

Legend

George and the Dragon

St George is famous for apparently slaying a dragon that was spreading a deadly plague through the city of Silene. This story was popularized in the thirteenth-century book *Golden Legend*.

The people of Silene gave the dragon sheep to eat to keep it away, and then when the animals ran out, they fed it children. The time came for the king's own daughter to be sacrificed, but before she was eaten, George, a wandering knight, rode past the lake where the dragon lived and killed it to save the princess.

Gorgon

- A gorgon is a female monster with snakes on her head instead of hair. It apparently also has hands made of brass and sharp fangs.

- The term gorgon comes from an ancient Indian word that means "gurgle" or "growl".

- The first-known images of gorgons appear in ancient Greek paintings from about 2,800 years ago.

- Ancient Greek myths say that the gorgons were three sisters: Stheno, Euryale, and Medusa. They were said to be the daughters of the sea god Phorcys and the sea monster Ceto.

- According to myth, all three gorgons could turn people to stone just by looking straight at them.

- Greek writer, Aeschylus, from the fifth century BCE, said Medusa lived on the island of Sarpedon, which was off the coast of what is now Turkey.

- Greek myths tell us that Stheno and Euryale were immortal, but Medusa was not. In the end she was killed by the famous Greek hero, Perseus.

Legend

Perseus and Andromeda

Medusa, the only mortal gorgon, was killed by Perseus. He could not look straight at her—or he would have been turned to stone. Instead, he watched her reflection in his shield, crept up on her in a cave where she slept, and chopped off her head with a sword. Medusa's head still had magical powers. Perseus kept it in his bag, and used it to turn his enemies to stone. When he heard that the sea god Poseidon had sent a monster to eat Andromeda, the princess of Ethiopia, he raced to save her. Perseus used Medusa's head to turn the sea monster into a huge rock in the sea.

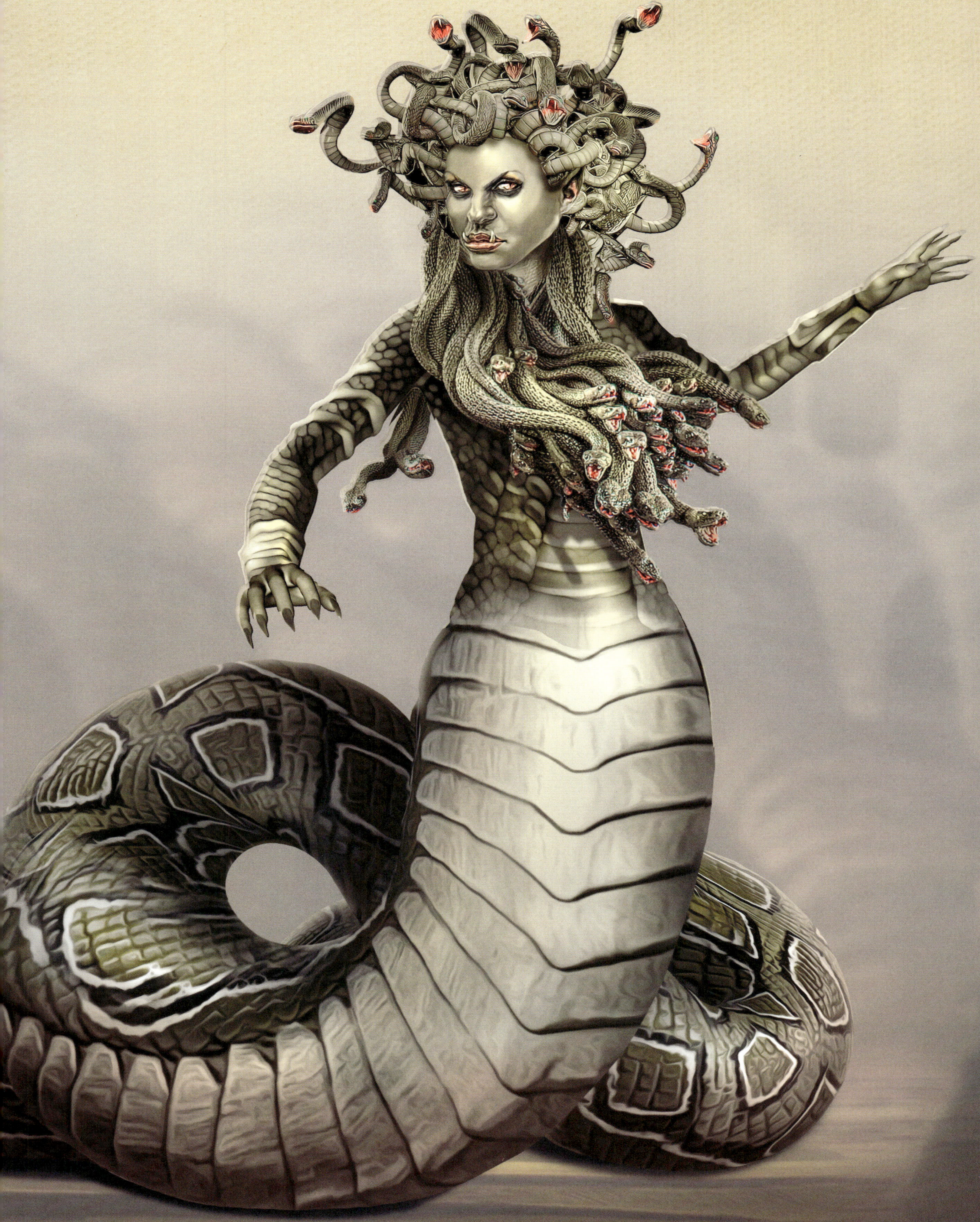

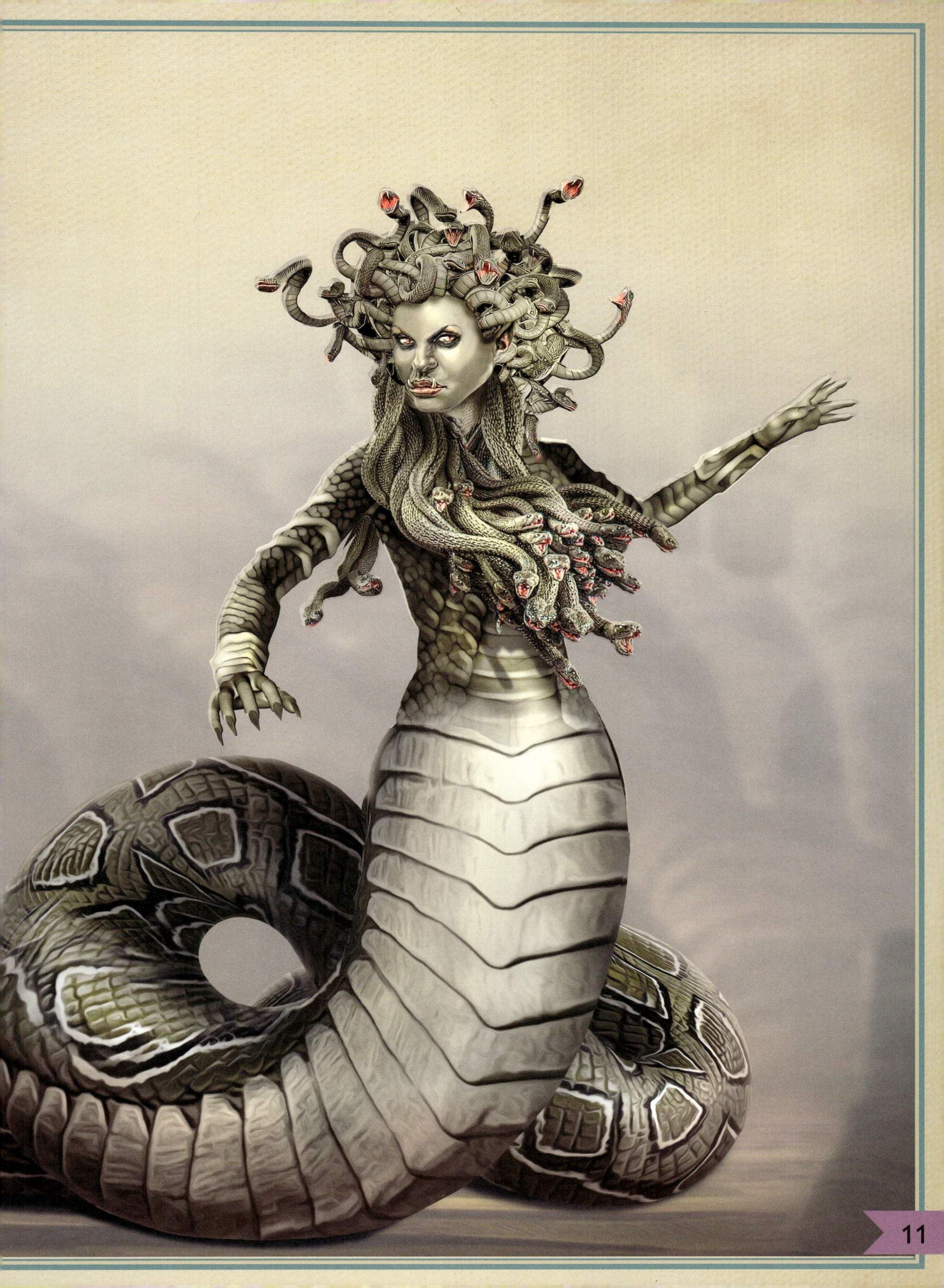

Kraken

- The kraken is a sea monster from the Arctic waters around Greenland. It was first described in Icelandic stories written in the thirteenth century.

- According to the stories, a kraken could swallow a ship whole.

- The word kraken comes from the Norwegian word for "twisted" or "crooked", and many have suggested that the monsters were actually giant squids seen by Viking explorers.

- *Örvar-Oddr*, an Icelandic story from the thirteenth century, says that the kraken was actually two monsters. One was a giant whale, while the other was a mass of mist with rocks for teeth.

Legend

Dangerous waters

Jacob Wallenberg, an eighteenth-century Swedish writer, said that the kraken stayed in deep water most of the time, and was always surrounded by a large shoal of fish. Fishermen came to the area to catch these fish in their nets, but needed to watch out. When the kraken came near the surface, the sea would apparently bubble and spray jets into the air, sinking the fishing boats. Wallenberg may be describing the eruption of an undersea volcano, which are quite common in the seas around Iceland.

- An old Norwegian book called *The King's Mirror*, written in 1250, said that the kraken was too large to breed and so there must only be one living the ocean.

- Erik Pontoppidan, a bishop who wrote a book about Norwegian animals in 1752, said that the kraken was so big that people thought it was an island!

- Carl Linnaeus, who created the system of classification (how all living things are ordered by scientists), added the kraken to his first book in 1735. He called it *Microcosmus marinus*, which means the "small world of the sea".

Giant

Giants are huge people—mostly men—that appear in myths and legends from all over the world. Unlike most other legendary monsters, giants look like people, but are much taller and stronger.

In Greek mythology, a race of giants went to war against the gods. The gods won largely because the hero Hercules, a man who was even stronger than the giants, fought on their side.

Nordic people believed that giants, known as the Jotnar, were the sworn enemies of the gods. Legend suggested that the world would end in a final battle between the two enemies.

Legend

Giant's Causeway

Legend has it that The Giant's Causeway, a formation of rocky pillars in Northern Ireland, once stretched all the way to Scotland. It was put there by the Irish giant Finn MacCool so that another giant from Scotland, called Benandonner, could walk over and fight him. However, Benandonner became scared and ran home, smashing the causeway into the sea.

In the twelfth century, Geoffrey of Monmouth told how the last British giant was called Gogmagog. He was thrown off a cliff by a giant called Corineus who arrived with the Roman invaders.

The Bible story of David and Goliath tells of a fight between a young shepherd (David) and a giant warrior (Goliath). David kept his distance from the giant and hurled a stone at his head using a sling-shot. Goliath was knocked out and David then killed him.

The most famous American giant is Paul Bunyan, a massive lumberjack, who, according to many nineteenth-century stories, travelled around the forests of North America performing great feats of strength.

Kelpie

- The kelpie is a Scottish water spirit that can change shape, and usually appears as a horse.

- Kelpies enticed people to climb on their backs for a ride, and then dived down under the water, drowning the rider.

- A kelpie normally looks like a horse but its hooves face backwards. However, the creature can also transform into other bodies, including a handsome young man.

- Kelpies are evil spirits and apparently responsible for causing dangerous rapids, whirlpools, and deadly floods in fast-flowing rivers.

- In 1810, the famous novelist Sir Walter Scott mentioned a kelpie in his poem *Lady of the Lake*. The kelpie demon creates a tornado-like water spout in the middle of a mountain lake.

- Modern experts believe that the idea of the kelpie comes from a fear of water at a time when many people lived by the coast but were unable to swim.

Legend

Loch Ness Monster

The most famous kelpie of all is the Loch Ness Monster. St Columba, an Irish monk, said that he had met a ferocious water beast on the bank of Loch Ness in 565 CE. The monster killed a man and so Columba apparently banished it to the depths of the lake. It was said that the fast currents that churned the waters of Loch Ness from time to time were from the kelpie swimming underneath. About 100 years ago, people started to think the Loch Ness Monster was actually a giant ancient reptile—although it has never been found.

Fairy

- Fairies are supernatural creatures that are included in British and Irish folktales. They also appear in stories from other European countries, but are given different names, such as pixies or brownies.

- In early stories, fairies were often described as being small, dark-haired people. They have wings which are often small and see-through like an insect's.

- Stories of fairies often say that they are kind and gentle creatures, but some can be evil—like the wicked Fairy Godmother in *Sleeping Beauty*.

- Fairies are said to nearly always stay out of sight. In Ireland, the myths explain that they lived inside ancient mounds (that were once used as burial grounds).

- A circle of mushrooms or toadstools growing in the forest is called a fairy ring. In medieval times, people believed that fairies gathered inside the ring to dance and cast spells. Anyone who stood in the ring would disappear!

Legend

Real fairies?

Arthur Conan Doyle, the author of stories about the clever detective Sherlock Holmes, was a great believer in fairies. In 1917, he saw a photograph that is now known as the *Cottingley Fairies*. It showed a little girl surrounded by tiny fairies. Conan Doyle was sure that this was evidence of these little creatures. However, in 1983 the girls who made the picture—now old women—admitted that they had simply cut out pictures and stuck them to plants. We are still waiting for the first picture of a real fairy!

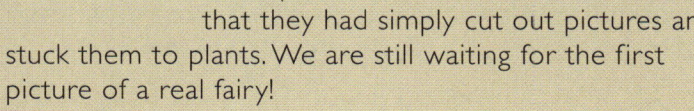

Children's stories of fantasy beasts of all kinds, and heroes and villains, are called fairy tales. They are modern versions of old stories that were used to teach children about the dangers of the world.

Ammit

- Ammit is an ancient Egyptian monster and goddess. Her name means "The Soul Eater".

- Paintings on papyrus from over 3,000 years ago show Ammit with the head of a crocodile, front legs and body of a lion, and rear end of a hippopotamus.

- According to the *Book of the Dead*, written in Egypt around 3,500 years ago, Ammit lived in the underworld beside a lake of fiery lava.

- Ancient Egyptians were terrified of Ammit because she could apparently stop them from reaching the afterlife.

- Other names for Ammit include "Eater of the Damned", "Devourer of Millions", and "Demoness of Death".

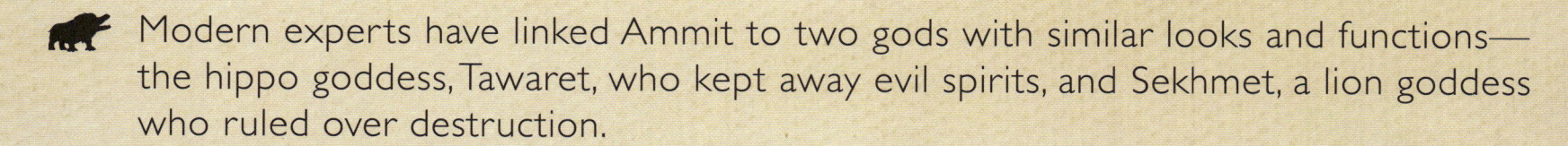

- Ammit lived with the gods but she was not a god herself. Instead, she was a powerful symbol of the power of the gods to punish people who did wrong.

- Modern experts have linked Ammit to two gods with similar looks and functions—the hippo goddess, Tawaret, who kept away evil spirits, and Sekhmet, a lion goddess who ruled over destruction.

Legend

Moment of judgement

As they were prepared for burial, ancient Egyptians had their hearts removed. It was believed that at the entrance of the underworld, their souls were tested by the jackal-headed god Anubis. The heart would be weighed on the Scales of Justice against a feather. Ammit sat beneath the scales and waited. If the heart was weighed down by too many bad deeds, Ammit would snatch it and eat it, and the person's soul would not be allowed into the afterlife.

Harpy

- Harpies were monstrous birds with the faces of human women. They are mentioned in many ancient Greek myths, including the Jason and the Argonauts.

- Ancient Greek pictures showed harpies as beautiful women, and according to myths they were the sisters of Iris, the goddess of rainbows.

- The phrase "snatched away by the harpies", meant that somebody had disappeared. Harpies were used to explain things that humans did not understand.

- According to the poems of the Greek writer, Homer, a sudden gust of wind is created by an approaching harpy.

Legend

Saved by the Argonauts

One of the stories in the ancient Greek myth of Jason and the Argonauts was about King Phineus. Zeus, the king of the gods, gave Phineus the power to see the future. However, Phineus told people about Zeus's secret plans, and so Zeus blinded him and sent him to live on an island. The island was full of food, but every time Phineus found some, harpies came and snatched it away. Phineus was finally rescued by Jason and his crew of sailors, the Argonauts. The crew included two men who could fly. They chased the harpies away and freed Phineus.

22

- Hesiod, another ancient Greek poet, said there were just two harpies: Aello (the whirlwind) and Ocypete (the swift wing). Later writers (such as Virgil) added a third harpy, Celano.

- Ancient Greeks called harpies, the "hounds of Zeus". Zeus was the king of the Greek gods, and legend has it that he sent harpies out to snatch up people who needed punishing.

- In ancient times, people thought that harpies carried evil people away to the Furies. The Furies were goddesses who punished people for their crimes by making them go insane.

Ogre

- An ogre is a large human-like monster that appears in European folktales. In stories, they often kidnap and eat people, especially children.

- The name ogre comes from the Etruscan god Orcus, the god of the underworld, who fed on human flesh. The Etruscans were the pre-Roman inhabitants of central Italy.

- The ogres in folktales are not only very tall and strong, but are also ugly. Some experts think that the idea for ogres came from many thousands of years ago, when ancient European people lived alongside Neanderthals, a larger form of humans.

- A book called *The History of the Kings of Britain*, that was written 900 years ago, says that ogres lived in Britain before humans arrived.

- Ogres are often described as having big teeth, bushy beards and eyebrows—and they smell really bad!

- In many European stories, ogres live alone in remote castles or lairs. They want to be left alone and become angry and dangerous when disturbed.

Legend

Puss in Boots

One of the most famous stories about an ogre is *Puss in Boots*, which was written around 1550. It tells the story of a clever cat who dresses up in human clothes and becomes wealthy and powerful. In one of the cat's adventures he outwits an ogre that can change into any shape. Puss in Boots convinces the huge ogre to become a tiny mouse—and the cat then pounces on him, and eats him!

25

Unicorn

- The unicorn is often seen as a symbol of unity and faithfulness.

- Ancient Greek writer, Ctesias, said a unicorn has a white body, purple head, blue eyes, and one long black horn with a red tip.

- The ancient Christian book, *Physiologus*, says a unicorn can purify a pool of dirty water simply by dipping its horn in.

- According to legend, the Throne Chair of Denmark was made of unicorn horn, or "alicorn". It was actually made of narwhal (whale) tusks, which were often sold as unicorn tusks.

Legend

Theories on catching a unicorn

Unicorns have traditionally been presented as being almost impossible to catch. Cosmas Indicopleustes, a Christian Egyptian of the sixth century CE, travelled in Africa and to India and reported about the strange creatures that he saw. He said that unicorns were always able to escape thanks to their strong horn. The unicorn would simply jump off a cliff to get away, it then turned in the air so that it landed on its horn, which would protect it from the fall.

- Roman writer Pliny the Elder described a unicorn as looking like a horse with the head of of stag, feet of an elephant, and the tail of a boar.

- Marco Polo thought that he saw a unicorn while travelling in Sumatra in the twelfth century CE, writing in his journal, "They have a single black horn in the middle of the forehead… They are very ugly brutes to look at." He was actually describing a rhinoceros.

Elf

- Elves appear in many myths from northern Europe, where they were believed to be beautiful human-like spirits.

- Ancient people believed that elves liked to be left alone, but would sometimes help humans in need.

- It was believed that elves gave people illnesses by firing tiny poison arrows at them.

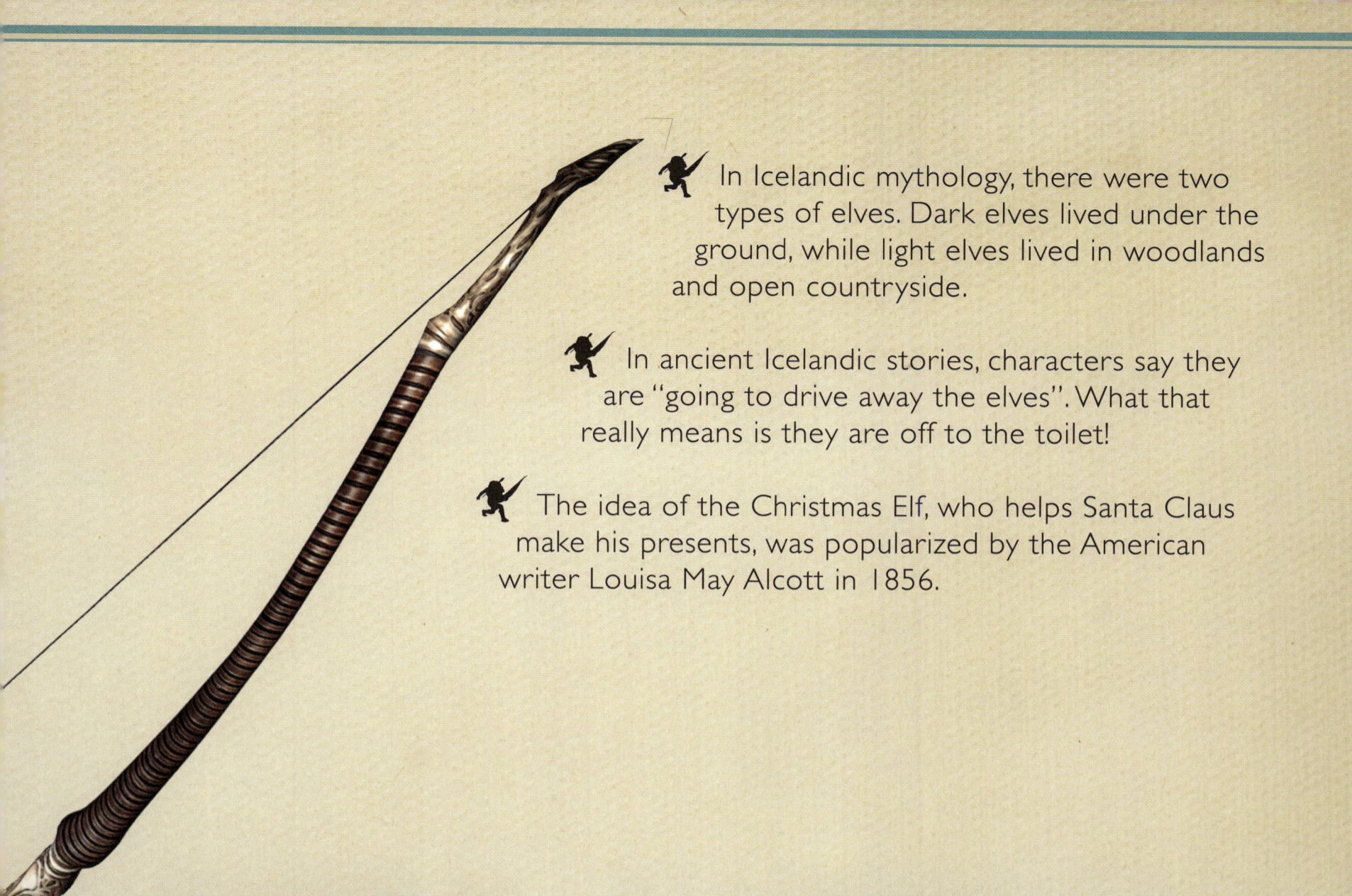

- In Icelandic mythology, there were two types of elves. Dark elves lived under the ground, while light elves lived in woodlands and open countryside.

- In ancient Icelandic stories, characters say they are "going to drive away the elves". What that really means is they are off to the toilet!

- The idea of the Christmas Elf, who helps Santa Claus make his presents, was popularized by the American writer Louisa May Alcott in 1856.

Legend

Pointy ears

Today, people imagine elves with pointy ears. This idea dates right back to Ancient Greek times and early traditions for wild creatures. Later, in the seventeeth century, pictures of Shakespeare's elf and fairy characters, such as Puck and Robin Goodfellow, are shown to have pointed ears. In nineteeth-century literature, the famous illustrator Arthur Rackham also presented his elves this way. More recently, this idea became popular when British author J R R Tolkein, wrote about elves in *The Hobbit* and *Lord of the Rings*. Tolkein based his elf characters on ancient myth, which said that elves were very much at home in woodlands and even had leaf-shaped ears.

Phoenix

- The phoenix is an immortal bird that appears in stories mostly from ancient Greece and Rome.

- All accounts say that the phoenix could renew itself. Once it had grown old it would die in a ball of flames. An egg would be in the ashes left behind, and a baby phoenix would hatch out.

Legend

Bennu

It is thought that the inspiration for the ancient Greek myth of the phoenix came from the similar Egyptian Bennu bird. According to Egyptian myths, the Bennu lived in the temple of Ra, the sun god, where it perched on a sacred pillar. When it had grown old, the Bennu apparently made a nest from cinnamon sticks and set them on fire. The Bennu turned to ashes from which a new bird arose. This new bird then formed the ash of its old body into an egg covered in a sticky resin and buried it.

- Many European cities would add a phoenix to their flags to show that they had once been destroyed long ago but had been rebuilt and were strong again.

- Pliny the Elder, a Roman writer, said that the phoenix was the size of an eagle. Others said it could live for 1,400 years before being reborn.

- Persian writer and famous Sufi (Muslim mystic) teacher, Hazrat Inayat Kahn, said that if a phoenix landed on your head it was a sign that you would one day be a king!

- In the Hindu religion, there is a similar legendary bird called Garuda, which was a flaming fire bird that pulled the chariot of the god Vishnu.

Bunyip

- A bunyip is a mythical creature that supposedly lives in rivers and billabongs, which are small, shallow lakes in Australia.

- The name bunyip means "devil" in a language used by Aboriginal Australians—the first people to live in that country.

- Australian myths most commonly describe bunyips as having dark fur, flippers instead of legs, the head of a dog with a duck's bill, and tusks like a walrus.

- In 1851, an Australian newspaper reported the discovery of ancient carvings that showed a creature that was possibly a bunyip.

- Aboriginal people believe that certain rocks and hills are the remains of bunyips and other ancient creatures that lived before humans arrived.

Legend

Bunyip sighting

In 1847, a bunyip was apparently spotted on a bank of the Yarra River near Melbourne's harbour. Some onlookers thought it was actually a giant duck-billed platypus. A team of men rowed over to take a look at the strange animal, but just as they got there, the creature slipped into the water and disappeared.

Some people think that bunyips are actually large elephant seals, which normally live near the South Pole, and sometimes get lost and swim up Australian rivers.

- Scientists have suggested that the idea for bunyips comes from giant marsupials (relatives of kangaroos) that have now become extinct (died out).

- In 1847, a strange skull was put on display at a museum in Sydney, Australia. At the time people thought it belonged to a bunyip, but experts confirmed it belonged to a deformed calf or foal.

33

Jinni

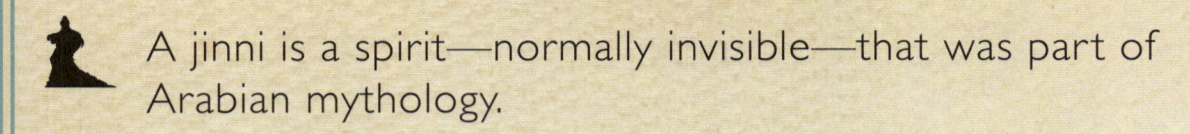

- A jinni is a spirit—normally invisible—that was part of Arabian mythology.

- In Middle Eastern traditions, a jinni watches over everybody, recording what they do and helping them to live good lives.

- It was possible for a jinni to be a bad influence, and it apparently whispered bad advice into people's ears.

Legend

Aladdin's lamp

The most famous story about a jinni comes from the renowned work *One Thousand and One Nights*, a collection of folktales and myths that was put together between the ninth and the thirteenth centuries. Antoine Galland, who translated the book into French in the eighteenth century, added some extra details of his own. One of these was that Aladdin made friends with a jinni trapped inside an oil lamp. When he rubbed the lamp, the jinni could escape—and promised to be Aladdin's servant. Early versions of Aladdin do not mention this.

- Jinn appear in Arabian stories, such as *One Thousand and One Nights*, written from the ninth century CE and reworked over time. They are said to be able to travel very fast—even flying between Arabia and China in an instant.

- In myths and stories from the Middle East and North Africa, a jinni can take any form—a person, an animal, a plant, or even appear as fire or a gust of wind.

- Although it is thought that jinn can take on any form, they are often shown in pictures as smoke-like figures with a head, body, and arms, but no legs.

Basilisk

- A basilisk is a legendary snake with the head of a cockerel. Some suggest it had legs, but no one can agree on how many—some say two, while others report six or even eight legs.

- In medieval times, the basilisk was believed to hatch when a cockerel brooded (kept warm) the egg of a snake.

- According to Roman writer Pliny the Elder's book *Natural History*, written in 79 CE, if a basilisk looked you straight in the eye, you would fall down dead.

- Pliny also explained that a basilisk's breath was so poisonous that it burned away the grass as it slithered along.

- The twelfth-century metalworker, Theophilus Presbyter, said he could make Spanish gold by mixing dried powdered basilisk with the blood of a red-headed man, melted red copper, and vinegar.

Legend

Rooster protection

The people of Cantabria in northern Spain have a myth that says that basilisks have died out across the rest of the world and only survive in their land. The terrifying creature is apparently scared of only one thing—the weasel. The smell of a weasel makes the basilisk slither away and hide. However, the only thing that can kill a basilisk, according to Cantabrian folklore, is the call of a cockerel—and so travellers would always carry a cockerel with them when they visited wild places.

- Pliny warned people not to kill a basilisk with a spear or a sword, as the poison would run though the weapon and kill you!
- A basilisk is not to be confused with a cockatrice, which is a dragon with a cockerel's head, which kills with a sting in its tail.

Gnome

Gnomes are earth spirits and appear in many European myths. Paracelsus, a Swiss alchemist (or wizard) from the sixteenth century, first gave them the name "gnome".

Paracelsus said that gnomes were ugly little people that lived underground—their name comes from the Greek for "earth dweller".

According to Paracelsus, gnomes could move through earth as easily as humans could move through air.

Gnomes were apparently very shy and stayed away from humans. If they met miners who were digging through their home, the gnome would make the tunnel collapse or explode.

Paracelsus said that gnomes were two spans tall. A span is the distance from the tip of the thumb to the tip of the little finger when the fingers are stretched wide.

Gnomes apparently wear pointed hats to make themselves look taller!

Gnomes are often grumpy and do not like humans digging up their stores of gold and jewels.

Legend

Garden gnomes

In the middle of the nineteenth century, gnomes started appearing in gardens, first in Germany and then across the world. They are apparently old gnomes who have grown tired of life underground. During the day, the gnomes stay completely still. At night they work on the garden, weeding the flowerbeds and keeping the plants healthy. It is said that as they work they tell each other sad stories.

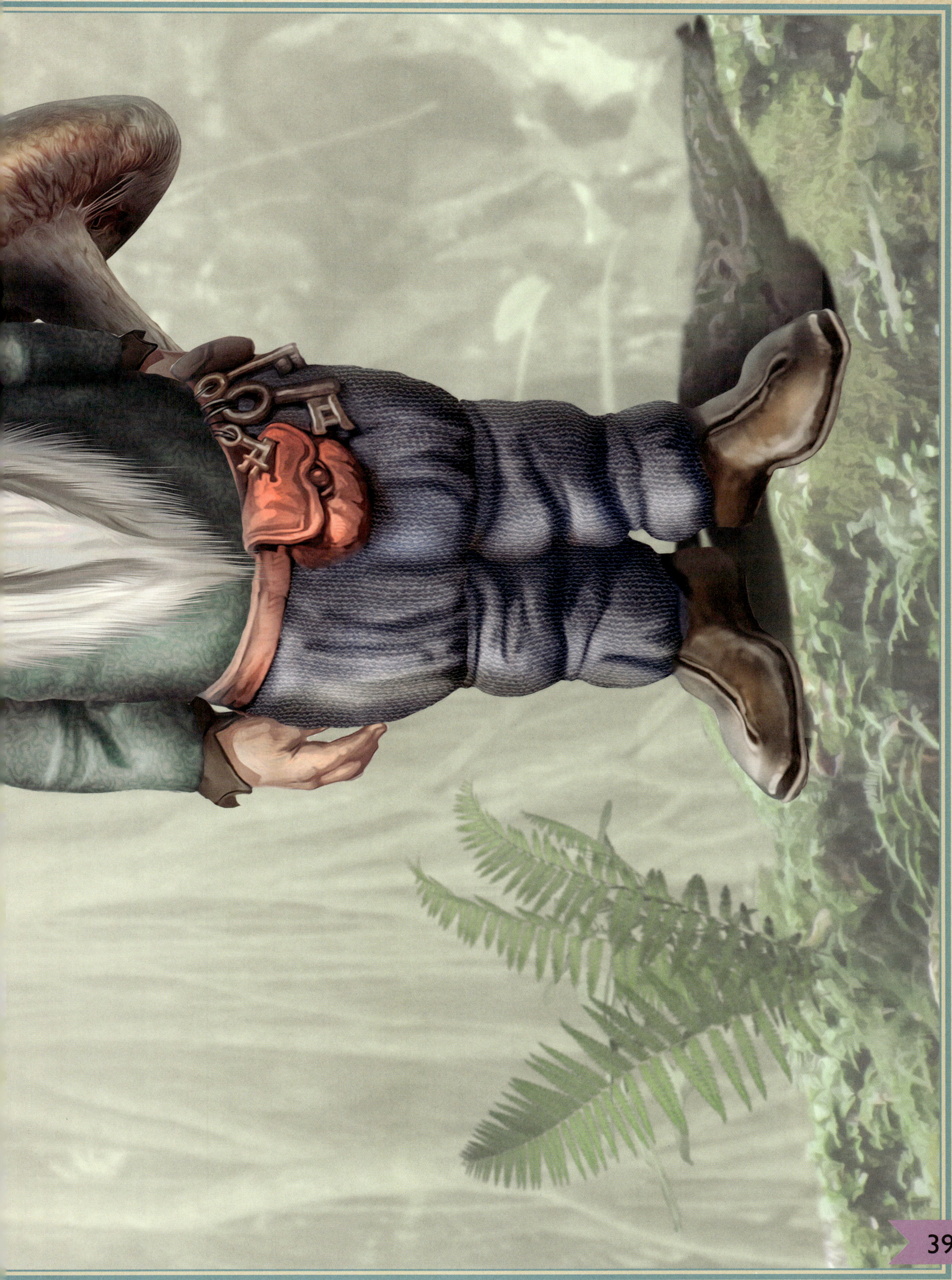

Mannegishi

- The Cree people of central Canada believe that they share the forest with little people called the Mannegishi.

- The mannegishi do not build houses but apparently live in the cracks between the rocks in river rapids. They carve pictures on rocks along river banks and in caves.

- Mannegishi have skinny bodies and very large heads with big eyes. They have no mouth or nose and have six fingers on each hand.

- The Cree say mannegishi are tricksters and like to crawl out of the rocks to capsize boats as they pass through rough waters.

- A mannegishi is often hard to spot but it is said that they make whining noises similar to the buzz of a dragonfly.

Legend

Dover Demon

The only record of anyone seeing a mannegishi was from 1977. A 17-year-old boy was driving home through Dover, Massachusetts, USA, and saw a creature with long fingers and glowing eyes standing on a wall above the road. The same night, the creature was seen by another boy running through woods nearby, and the following night a girl saw it sitting by the road. All three drew a picture of what they had seen showing a monkey-shaped body without hair and a very big head. When they told their stories, many people believed it was a mannegishi, but others said it could have been a baby moose.

- According to the Cree myth, a mannegishi can breathe air and also absorb oxygen through the skin when underwater.

- The Objiwa people who live further south in Canada than the Cree, also believe in little creatures that live near rivers—they call them memegwesi.

Banshee

- According to Irish folklore, a banshee is a female spirit that appears and gives out a high-pitched wail as a warning that a family member is about to die.

- In Gaelic (Irish language) books and songs, a banshee typically wears a green dress, a grey cloak, and she has long, tangled red hair that shimmers like fire.

- The name banshee comes from the Irish for "woman of the mound". This refers to the ancient burial mounds or rounded hills that are seen across the Irish countryside.

- Some traditional Irish songs explain that the main clans of Ireland are said to have their own banshees who follow them all over the world.

- The O'Brian clan's chief banshee is said to be called Aoibheall. She is believed to live by a large rock, Craig Liath, that sits beside the River Shannon in southwest Ireland.

- Irish folklore explains that if you meet a wailing banshee you are about to enter a deadly situation. Your death is not certain, as long as you heed the banshee's warning.

- In Scottish stories, banshees are called *bean nighe*, which means "little washerwoman". They are apparently seen by rivers washing the clothes of those who are about to die in battle.

Legend

The death of James I of Scotland

James I of Scotland, who ruled in the fifteenth century, was assassinated by rival nobles who disputed his right to the throne. He was murdered at a monastery in Perth, Scotland.

Stories of this assassination tell how James was approached by an old woman as he crossed a river to reach the monastery, where he was staying that night. She repeatedly warned him that he would not come out alive, but he ignored her. At the time many people believed that the king had been warned by a banshee.

43

Griffin

- A griffin has the body of a lion and the head and wings of an eagle. The oldest pictures found of griffins were drawn 5,000 years ago in ancient Egypt.

- The kings of Susa, an ancient kingdom in what is now western Iran, sealed their letters with wax stamped with a griffin symbol. That symbol showed the letter was true and important.

- In ancient Greece, the griffin was a symbol of power because it combined the king of beasts, the lion, with the king of birds, the eagle.

- The Roman poet Virgil, who lived in the first century BCE, wrote about a new kind of griffin called the hippogriff, which was half eagle and half horse.

Legend

Powerful beasts

The Travels of Sir John Mandeville is a memoir of a fictional English explorer who travelled through North Africa and Asia in the fourteenth century. It is based on the experiences of genuine travellers at that time. Mandeville said that griffins were most common in Bacharia, a land that was in what is now Afghanistan. He said that one griffin had the strength of ten lions and a hundred eagles, and could carry an entire horse through the air to its nest. The griffin's claws were apparently longer than a bull's horns, and the feathers were strong enough to make bows for firing arrows.

- The medieval kings of Europe collected "griffin claws", which were actually carved antelope horns, and "griffin eggs", which were actually ostrich eggs.

- Philostratus, a Greek philosopher from 200 CE, suggested that griffins were used to mine gold in India, where they dug out nuggets with their strong beaks.

Troll

- According to Viking myths, trolls are ugly creatures that live in the steep, rocky mountains of Scandinavia.

- Scandinavian stories explain that trolls are not very clever and are slow-moving. However, they are very strong.

- In ancient times, people believed that sunlight turned trolls to stone, and so they only moved around during the night.

- In Swedish folklore, trolls steal food from farms, and during the winter they sneak into houses at night and eat and drink whatever they can find.

- Ancient Scandinavians were scared of trolls, fearing that they would kidnap them and even eat them!

- In Scandinavian folklore, Thor protected humans from trolls by throwing his magical hammer at them, which sent out bolts of lightning to kill trolls.

Legend

Three Billy Goats Gruff

This tale comes from Norway, and was first written down in the 1840s. It tells of a greedy troll who was living in a river under a bridge, and was tricked by three goats. One goat is a young kid, the other is the mother goat, while the third is a big, strong billy goat, or the father goat. When the kid crosses the bridge the troll threatens to eat it, but the kid suggests waiting for its mother, who is bigger. The mother goat does the same, telling the troll to eat the big billy goat, which would make a better meal. However, the billy goat is strong enough to fight off the troll, who is washed away by the river, and all three goats escape.

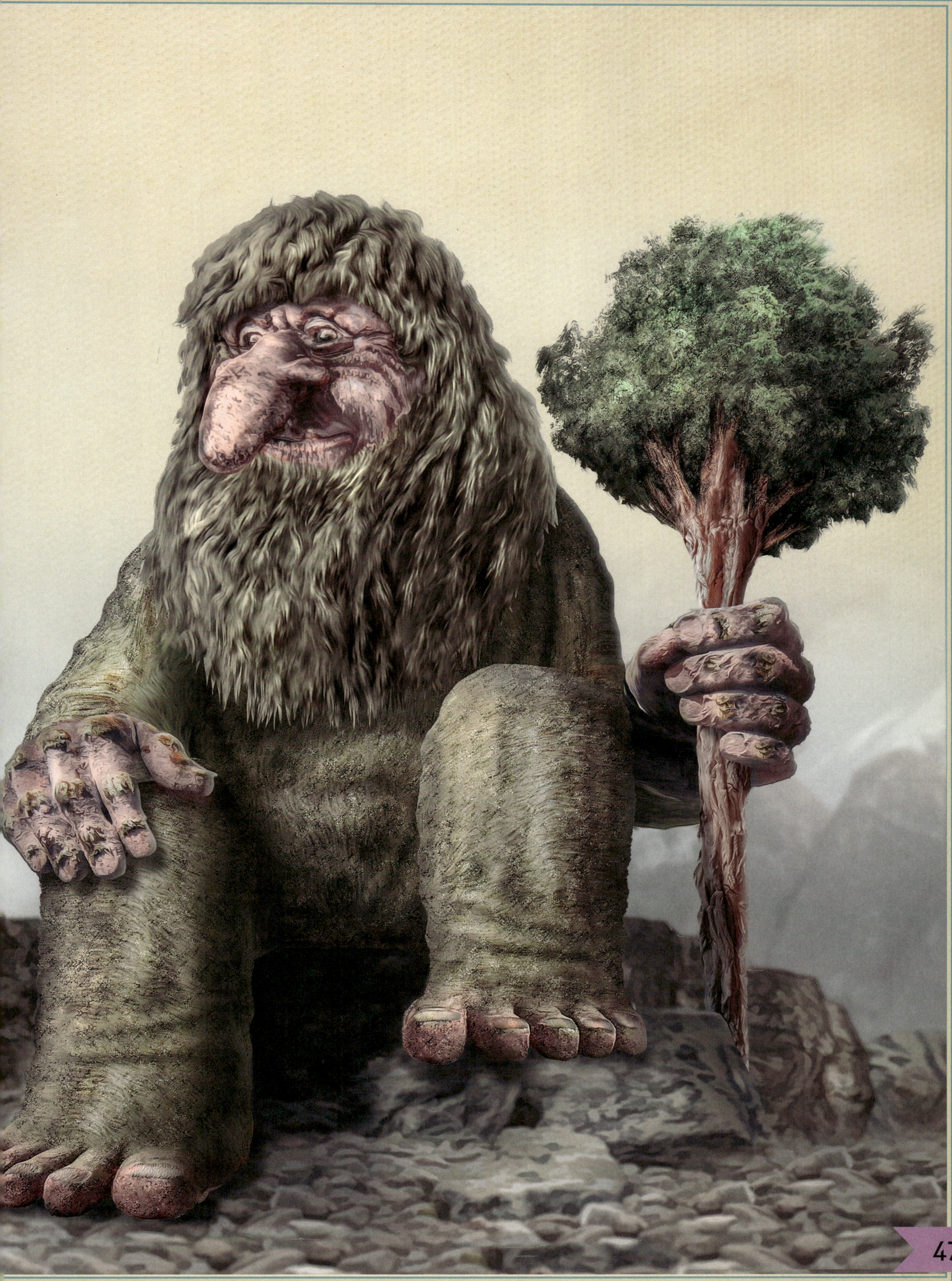

Jorogumo

- Jorogumo is a spider demon from Japanese stories told in the seventeenth century.

- The stories say that the demon can transform from a giant spider into a beautiful woman who lures wandering travellers, often lonely samurai warriors.

- In the seventeeth century, Japanese people believed that Jorogumo would play a lute to get the attention of travellers in the middle of dense forests.

- As a woman, Jorogumo often carries a baby, but when she transforms into a spider again, the baby becomes her egg sac.

- After enticing her victims, Jorogumo ties them up in her web—and eats them. Her name means "tying bride" in Japanese.

Legend

Home of Jorogumo

According to Japanese tradition, Jorogumo is said to live at Joren Falls, in southern Japan. A folktale says that a woodcutter was resting by the waterfall, and silk threads appeared from the water and wrapped around his legs. He cut the threads with his axe and tied them around a tree. The threads then pulled the tree into the water. Local people became frightened of the waterfall, but travellers passing the water would often fall in love with Jorogumo and would never be seen again.

- Jorogumo is also the name of a large type of spider that lives in Japan and spins webs with golden silk.
- As well as being an evil spirit, Jorogumo is also thought to protect people from drowning. Many waterfalls in Japan have a shrine to her.

Thunderbird

- The myths of Native American peoples include that of a giant eagle that creates the sound of thunder by flapping its wings.

- The legend of the Menominee people of Wisconsin, USA, explains that thunderbirds live on a mountain that floats high above the clouds.

- In Algonquian myths, the thunderbirds rule the sky and protect the Earth from a horned snake that allegedly lives underground and an evil panther that lives in the sea.

- The Objibwe people of eastern Canada believe that thunderbirds are most active in the summer when they fight off evil water spirits that create strong winds and rainstorms.

- Thunderbirds appear at the top of traditional totem poles. They are not like ordinary eagles because they have horns and teeth.

Legend

The Wakinyan

The Lakota Sioux tribe from the western United States tell of four great thunderbirds, called the Wakinyan, which they believe arrive with migrating birds in spring. The chief thunderbird crosses from the west. His black body is hidden in clouds with only his beak, claws, and long wings sticking out. The red wakinyan comes from the north, and a yellow thunderbird comes from the east. The white thunderbird arrives from the south and has no eyes or ears, but can still see and hear!

- According to many Native American traditions, flashes of lightning are caused by thunderbirds blinking and lightning bolts are the birds throwing snakes to the ground.

- Shaman, who were said to have healing powers, catch glimpses of parts of these great beasts in their dreams. However, they never see a complete thunderbird all at once.

Mermaid

✤ On his second voyage to America in 1493, Christopher Columbus reported seeing three mermaids leaping from the water—but he said they were not as beautiful as the pictures he had seen.

✤ *Sirenia* is the scientific name for water-living mammals like manatees, which have two front legs, or arms, but no back legs and a paddle-shaped tail. These animals may have been mistaken for mermaids by sailors.

✤ The Greek philosopher Anaximander from the sixth century BCE, suggested that humans had evolved from mermaids.

✤ The Duala people, living near the coast of Cameroon, Africa, believe that mermaids called the Miengu swim up rivers to carry messages from their dead ancestors, who live under the sea.

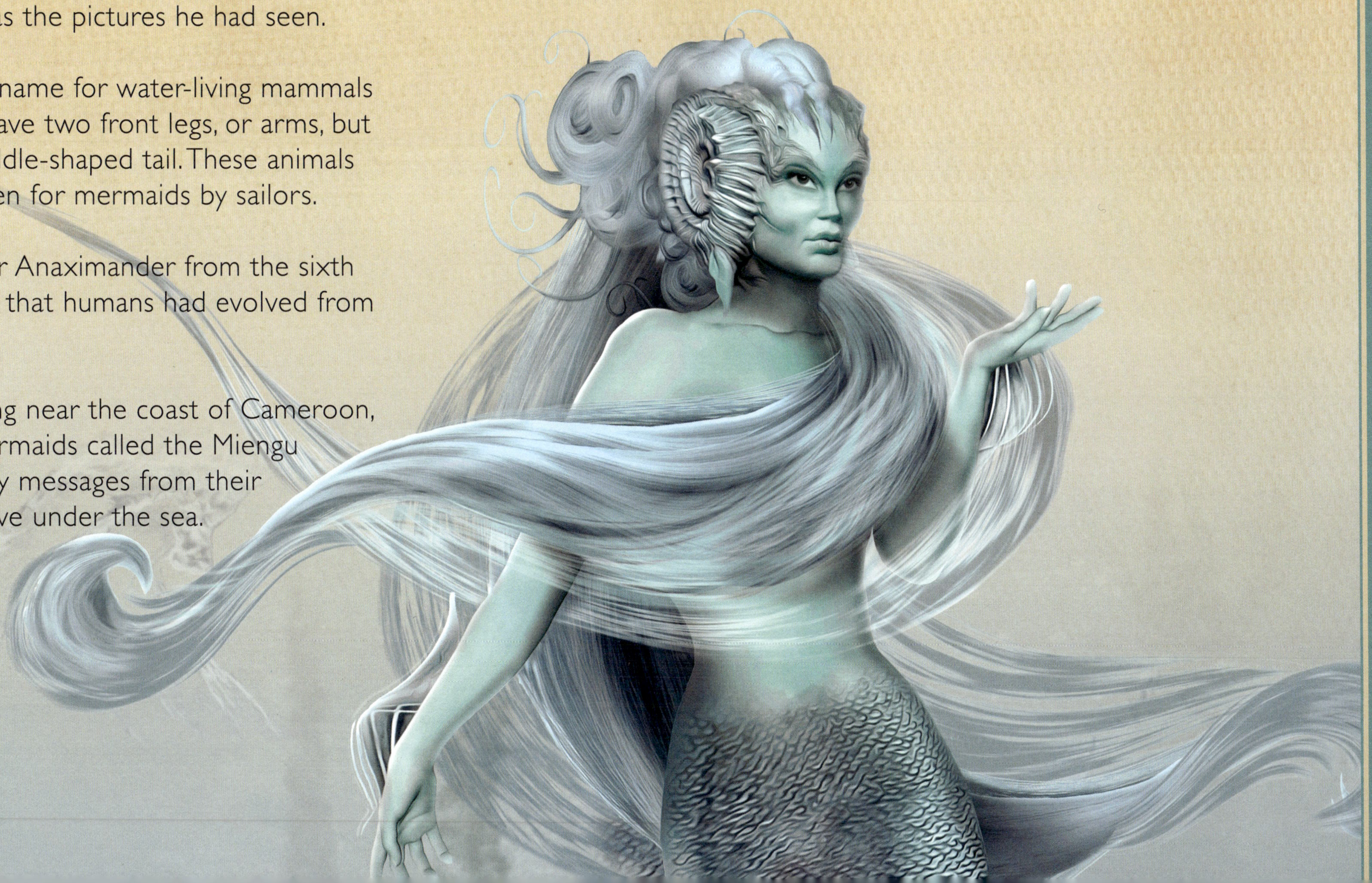

Legend

The first mermaid?

The earliest story of a mermaid is from about 3,000 years ago and comes from Assyria, in what is now Iraq. A beautiful goddess called Atargatis killed her lover by mistake and was so sad that she jumped into a lake and turned herself into a fish. However, she could not hide her great beauty and became half human and half fish.

The eighteenth-century pirate, Blackbeard, was scared of mermaids. He always steered his ship away from areas where mermaids had apparently been spotted.

53

Minotaur

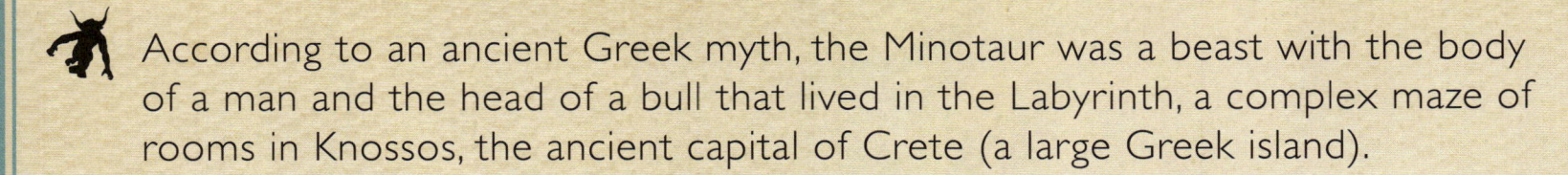

- According to an ancient Greek myth, the Minotaur was a beast with the body of a man and the head of a bull that lived in the Labyrinth, a complex maze of rooms in Knossos, the ancient capital of Crete (a large Greek island).

- The Labyrinth may have been a description of the palace of King Minos, which was one of the largest and most elaborate buildings in Europe about 3,500 years ago.

- According to the Roman poet Ovid, who lived 2,000 years ago, the Labyrinth was built by Greek sculptor, Daedalus, with help from his son Icarus. Their design was so complex, that even they could not find the way out when it was finished!

- To escape from the Labyrinth—and the Minotaur within—Daedalus built wings from feathers and wax so that he and Icarus could fly home. However, Icarus flew too high, and his wings melted, so he fell to his death.

- King Minos demanded that Aegeus, the leader of Athens, give him seven boys and seven girls every seven years—and he fed them to the Minotaur.

Legend

Killing of the Minotaur

The story of how Theseus killed the Minotaur is an important myth in the history of the city of Athens. Theseus, the son of King Aegeus, one of the early kings of Athens, decided to go to the Labyrinth to stop the Minotaur killing Athenians. When he arrived, Ariadne, King Minos's daughter, gave him a long ball of string to unwind through the Labyrinth. Theseus killed the Minotaur and followed the string out of the maze. He had told his father that he would hoist a white sail on his ship for his safe return to Athens, but Theseus forgot his promise. When Aegeus saw the black sail approaching, he threw himself off a cliff into the sea. The sea around Greece is named after him—the Aegean.

The Minotaur myth is thought to be based on an ancient religion, where people worshipped Moloch. Moloch was shown as a large metal statue of a bull. Fires raged in the hollow centre of the statue—and children were said to be thrown inside as sacrifices for the god!

Cerberus

- Cerberus was a huge dog that guarded the entrance to the underworld, the land of the dead, according to ancient Greek myths.

- Cerberus had more than one head, but different writers gave him a different number. He is normally shown with three heads, but Pindar, a Greek writer from 2,450 years ago, insisted that he had 100 heads!

- Apollodorus, a Greek writer from the second century CE, said that as well as three heads, Cerberus also had a mane of snakes growing out of his neck!

- Roman poet Ovid, said that Cerberus had a venomous bite like a snake.

Legend

Captured by Hercules

Hercules, a strong hero from Greek myths, was given 12 impossible tasks by his king as a punishment. For his final task, he had to capture Cerberus and bring him to the king. Hades, the god of the underworld, said Hercules could take the dog, but only if he captured him without using a shield or metal weapons. Hercules used the thick skin of a lion to protect himself from Cerberus's bites. As Hercules dragged Cerberus through the land, his dog spit dripped on the ground making poisonous plants called wolfsbane sprout from the ground.

56

- Hesiod, who wrote down many ancient Greek myths in the eighth century BCE, recorded that Cerberus was the son of two serpent beasts, Typhon and Echidna—and was the brother of other monsters such as the Hydra, Chimera, and the gorgons.

- Hesiod explained that Cerberus ate any dead person who tried to escape from the underworld back to the land of the living.

- Cerberus apparently had a brother called Orthrus. Orthrus had just two heads and was the guard dog of the three-headed giant called Geryon.

Ghoul

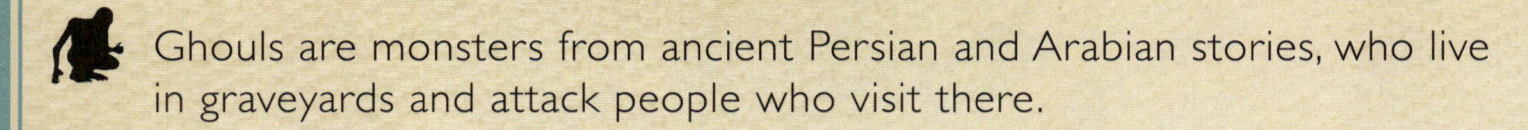

- Ghouls are monsters from ancient Persian and Arabian stories, who live in graveyards and attack people who visit there.

- The word ghoul comes from an Arabic word which means "to seize".

- People believed that ghouls could take the form of hyenas and would attack travellers moving through desert areas.

- According to Islamic tradition, a ghoul is a spirit, or jinn, controlled by the devil.

- It was believed ghouls drank the blood of the living and ate the bodies of the dead.

- A ghoul could apparently change its shape, and took on the appearance of the last dead person that it had eaten.

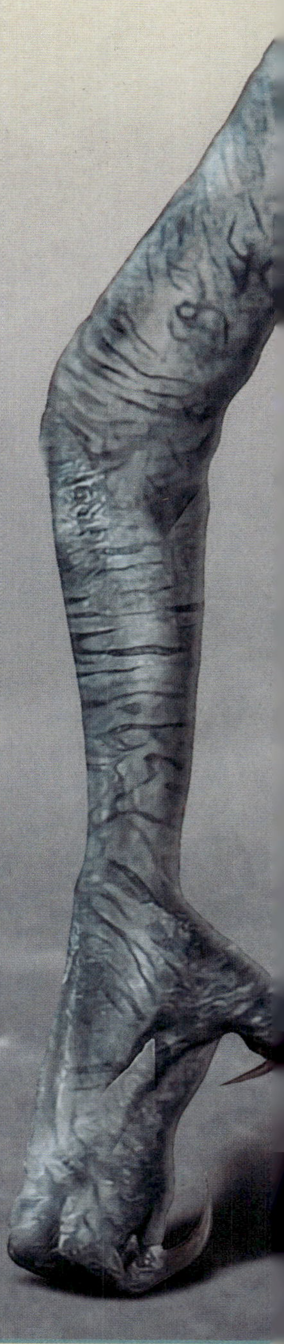

Legend

Demon Star

Algol is a bright star that can be seen in the night's sky. It's name comes from the Arabic "al ghūl" which means "the ghoul". Arab astronomers saw that this star changed its brightness, growing dim and then getting brighter again every few days. They were disturbed by this and thought it was ruled by a demon. In 1783, teenage astronomer, John Goodricke, discovered that Algol's strange light was in fact two stars. A small, dim star moved in front of the larger one every four days, blocking out its light. When the small star moved away, the brighter one's light reappeared.

Ghouls appear in many of the stories contained in *One Thousand and One Nights*, a collection of myths and folktales that was put together between the ninth and the thirteenth centuries in Iraq, and which has been added to over centuries.

Chimera

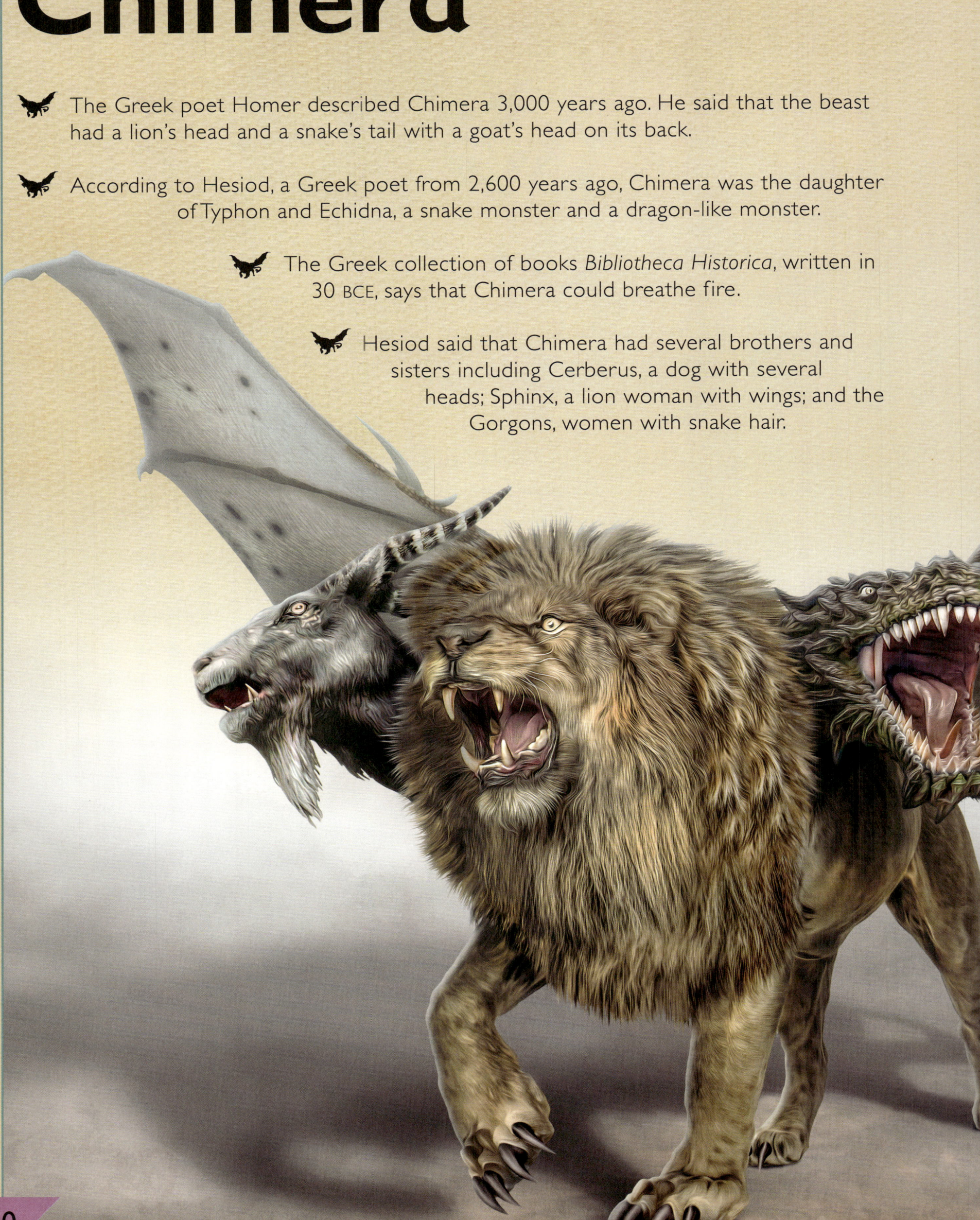

- The Greek poet Homer described Chimera 3,000 years ago. He said that the beast had a lion's head and a snake's tail with a goat's head on its back.

- According to Hesiod, a Greek poet from 2,600 years ago, Chimera was the daughter of Typhon and Echidna, a snake monster and a dragon-like monster.

- The Greek collection of books *Bibliotheca Historica*, written in 30 BCE, says that Chimera could breathe fire.

- Hesiod said that Chimera had several brothers and sisters including Cerberus, a dog with several heads; Sphinx, a lion woman with wings; and the Gorgons, women with snake hair.

60

🦇 Mount Chimaera is a volcano in western Turkey, once the ancient kingdom of Lycia. Hot gases leak from the rocks there and catch fire. Roman writer Pliny the Elder suggested that the myth of Chimera was inspired by this mountain.

🦇 All stories of Chimera say that she did a lot of damage. Whenever she appeared, people knew that a disaster, such as a storm, earthquake, or volcanic eruption, was likely soon.

Legend

Death of Chimera

Lobates, the king of Lycia (which is now in western Turkey), ordered the hero Bellerophon to kill Chimera. Bellerophon was able to do so by flying above Chimera on the winged horse Pegasus, so he could stay out of reach of the monster's fiery breath. Homer explained that Bellerophon then dropped a lump of lead into Chimera's throat and her red-hot breath melted the metal, which then burned through her insides.

Yeti

- The Yeti allegedly lives in the Himalayan mountains in southern Asia. The name "Yeti" comes from the Tibetan words for "rock bear".

- In 1921, British explorer Charles Howard-Bury visited the mountains and saw footprints in the snow. His guide said that they belonged to Kang-mi, which translates to the Abominable Snowman.

- The people of the Himalayas are mainly Buddhist today, but about 1,300 years ago they believed in many spirits, including the Yeti, or a wild hunter that lived high in the snowy peaks.

- In 2000, an Italian mountaineer wrote a book about how he met a Yeti in the Himalayas. He said the creature was actually a species of giant brown bear that can walk on its back legs.

Legend

Yeti specimens

Over the years, mountaineers have found scraps of fur and bone in the Himalayas that they claim have come from a Yeti. DNA tests show that these are actually from bears or mountain goats. However, in 1954 Yeti specimens were discovered at Pangboche Monastery in Nepal. One was a bone covered in hair and was thought to be from the animal's head. The hairs resembled those of an ape. The other specimen looked like hand bones. The best place to test what became known as the "Pangboche hand" at that time was England. A series of tests finally revealed that the bones were human and not from a Yeti at all!

There are reports of large ape-like creatures living in mountain ranges all over the world. A famous one is Bigfoot, from the forested mountains of western North America.

In the 1960s, Bhutan, a small Himalayan kingdom, issued a stamp showing a picture of the Yeti because Bhutanese people celebrated it as part of their culture.

In 1983, American Yeti-hunters explored the Barun Valley in Nepal, where many large footprints had already been found. They heard reports from local people about strange animals that lived in trees—these were probably Asiatic black bears.

Lóng Dragon

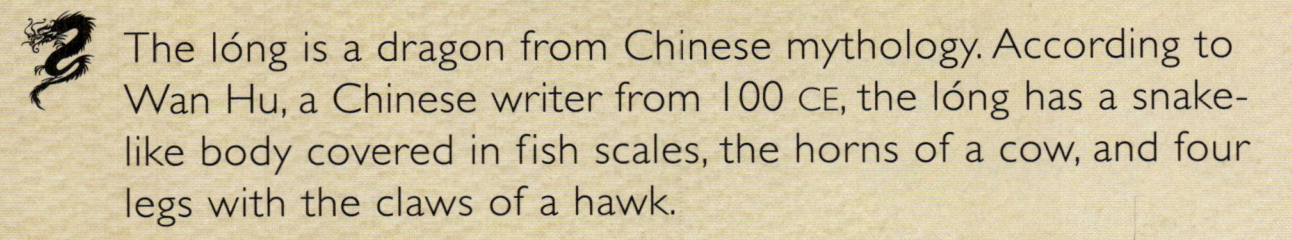

- The lóng is a dragon from Chinese mythology. According to Wan Hu, a Chinese writer from 100 CE, the lóng has a snake-like body covered in fish scales, the horns of a cow, and four legs with the claws of a hawk.

- Unlike legendary dragons from other parts of the world, Chinese people believe a lóng brings them good luck.

- The yellow lóng was the symbol of all Chinese emperors. Chinese folklore says that this creature lived in the Yellow River, which runs through the country.

- Skyscrapers in Hong Kong often have "dragon holes", or spaces in the middle of the building, so they do not block the path of invisible lóng spirits that fly down from the mountains to the sea.

Legend

The Four Seas

The borders of ancient China—before it became a single kingdom 2,200 years ago—were marked by the "Four Seas": The East China Sea, the South China Sea, Lake Baikal in the north, and Lake Qinghai in the west. It is believed that each of the "seas" was ruled by a powerful lóng, known as the dragon kings.

In times of drought, the dragon kings apparently flew into the sky making great rain clouds, which refilled the rivers.

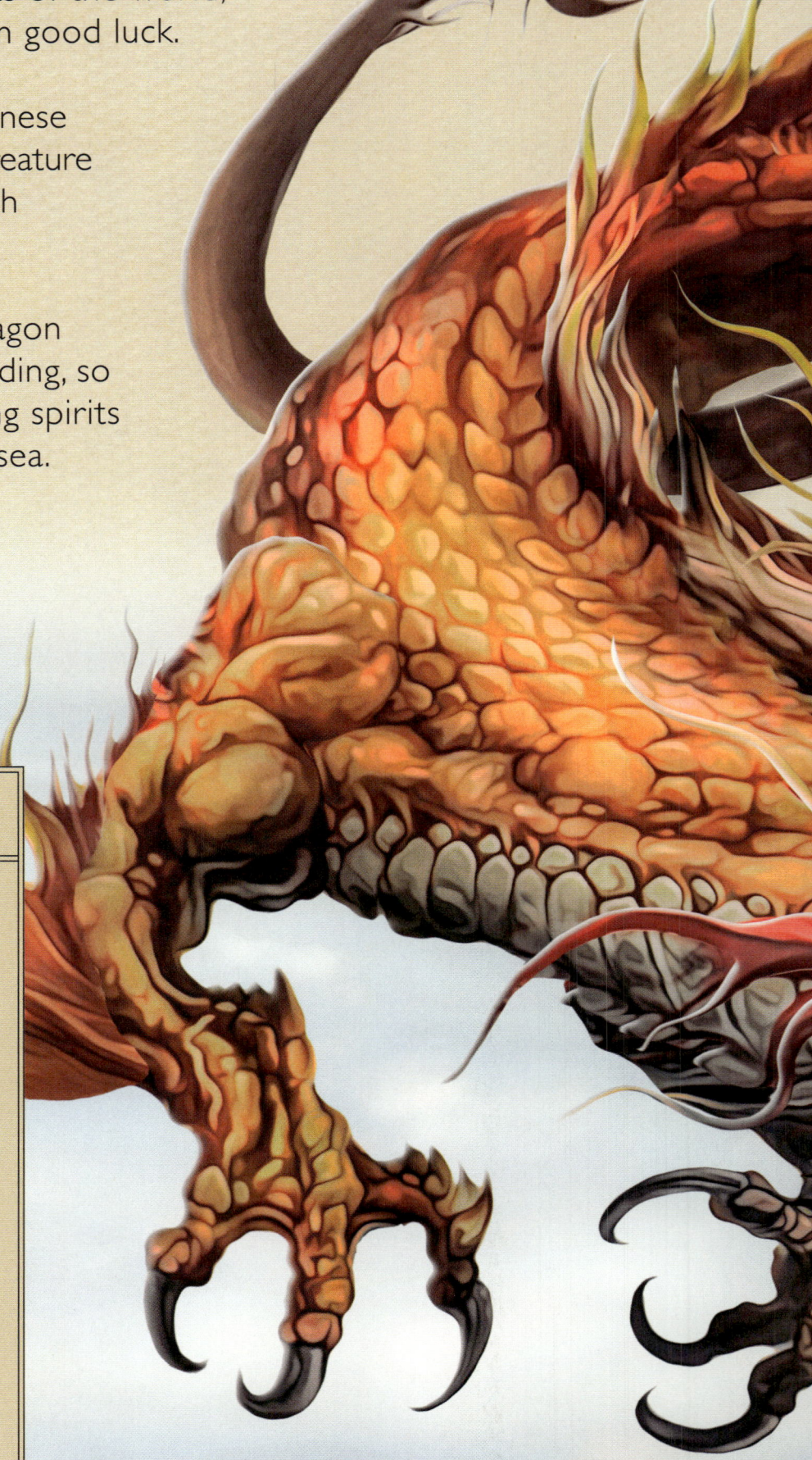

The people of Bhutan believe that thunder is the roar of Druk, a lóng that apparently lives in the sky above their mountainous country.

According to Chinese tradition, the lóng's enemy is the tiger. They are equal rivals but the lóng fights using intelligence, while the tiger uses its strength.

Cyclops

- A cyclops is a monster mentioned in several ancient Greek myths. It is a man-like giant with one eye in the middle of the forehead.

- According to the Greek poet Hesiod, who lived 2,600 years ago, there were just three cyclops: Brontes, Steropes, and Arges, who were the sons of the sky god and earth goddess.

- Hesiod explained that the three cyclops were expert craftsmen, who built armour and weapons for Zeus, the king of the gods.

- The name cyclops means "round eye" in Greek.

- The poet Homer, suggested there was a whole community of cyclops. They were shepherds who lived on remote islands and were the children of Poseidon, the sea god.

- The ancient city of Tiryns in Greece was mostly a ruin by around 1100 BCE. Local people believed its huge walls and maze of tunnels had been built by the cyclops.

- Many stories, including the play *Cyclops*, written in 408 BCE by Euripides, tell how cyclops were very dangerous and liked to eat people.

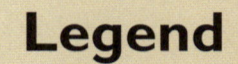

Legend

Escaping the cyclops

Homer's famous story, the *Odyssey*, tells the story of Odysseus and his men who were captured by a cyclops called Polyphemus while they were resting in a cave. The cyclops began to gradually eat Odysseus's crew, two at a time. One night, Odysseus gave Polyphemus a powerful wine that made him fall asleep. The crew then blinded him by driving a large stick into his single eye. The next day, Polyphemus let his sheep out of the cave. However, Odysseus and his men had tied themselves under the sheep and managed to escape undetected.

Amphisbaena

- An amphisbaena was a snake-like creature from ancient Greek myths that had a head at each end of its body.

- Medieval pictures and sculptures show the amphisbaena with chicken's feet, feathered wings—and sometimes with one head eating the other.

- The word "amphisbaena" means "go both ways", because it was not possible to tell which end was the head and which was the tail.

- Roman writer, Pliny the Elder, writing in the first century CE, said that the amphisbaena was doubly dangerous because venom could come out of both its mouths.

- According to the second-century-BCE Greek physician Nicander, wrapping the skin of an amphisbaena around a walking stick would keep other snakes from attacking you as you walked past them.

- Lumberjacks were said to nail the skin of a dead amphisbaena to a tree. This weakened the tree, making it easier to cut down with an axe.

Legend

Born from blood

According to Greek mythology, the amphisbaena had been born from a drop of blood that fell from the head of Medusa, the gorgon, as her killer Perseus flew over the desert of Libya (in North Africa) on his winged horse. Cato, a Roman general, reported seeing an amphisbaena as he led his army through the desert during the Roman civil war in the first century BCE.

An unusual kind of real-life burrowing reptile is named the amphisbaenan—or worm lizard. These animals are closely related to lizards but have no legs like a snake. Their heads are only tiny so it is hard to tell which end it is at.

Vampire

- A vampire is an immortal being that is believed to kill people by drinking their blood. The idea of a vampire is an ancient one, and has been recorded in ancient myths from the Middle East, India, and Europe.

- In medieval Europe, people believed that vampires had bloated bodies and purple skin from all the blood they drank. They also had untidy hair, long nails, and blood around their mouths and noses.

- In the nineteenth century, the idea of vampires changed. Vampires were seen to be thin and pale if they had not had a meal of blood, and they had long fangs for piercing the skin.

- The Slavic people of eastern Europe believed that vampires spent the daytime in graves and came out at night to feed around graveyards.

- European tradition says that the only way to stop a vampire is to drive a wooden stake through their heart.

- Europeans believed there were several ways of keeping a vampire away. These included carrying garlic, sprinkling mustard seeds on the roof of your house, or putting mirrors on doors—many believed a vampire did not reflect in a mirror.

Legend

Count Dracula

In 1897 the Irish author Bram Stoker wrote the book *Dracula*. It became the most famous vampire story ever. Stoker's story tells how Count Dracula, a vampire from Transylvania—a region of Europe, now Romania—came to England to find fresh victims. Every time he attacked a person, they would become a vampire too. Professor Van Helsing goes to help the victims and Dracula is eventually killed. Stoker's story is made up, but it was based on a real-life Romanian count, called Vlad Dracula, who was a violent warlord in the fifteenth century. Stories about the way he would torture his enemies have led Vlad Dracula to be better known as Vlad the Impaler.

Hydra

- The hydra was a many-headed snake-like monster that lived in a swamp at Lerna, a place filled with springs and caves in southern Greece.

- Ancient Greeks believed that Lerna was one of the entrances to the underworld, and that the Hydra was the daughter of two monsters that lived under the ground.

- Bronze jewellery made in ancient Greece around 700 BCE, shows a picture of the Hydra with six heads.

- Euripedes, writing in around 400 BCE, said that if you cut off one of the Hydra's heads, two more would grow back in its place—and so the Hydra had developed dozens, even as many as fifty, heads!

- According to Greek myths, the Hydra's breath was deadly and even the smell of its breath could kill.

- A book from the fourth century CE, *On Unbelievable Tales*, suggests that the Hydra was really a mother snake surrounded by her young.

Legend

Hercules slays the Hydra

The story of the hero Hercules is told in Hesiod's book *Theogony* from 2,700 years ago. Hercules was sent on a mission to perform 12 tasks, which were thought to be impossible. One of these tasks was to kill the Hydra. Hercules covered his nose and mouth so that the monster's breath and smell would not affect him. As he cut off each head, Hercules scorched the neck with a flaming torch. This stopped new heads from growing back. Eventually, the Hydra had just one head left, and Hercules used a bronze sword to slice it off.

An older myth from 4,000 years ago in Mesopotamia—which is now Syria and Iraq—tells of a seven-headed snake-like creature called Musmahhu that lived in the mountains.

Centaur

🐎 A centaur has the head, body, and arms of a man which are connected to the body of a horse.

🐎 According to the ancient poet Homer, the first centaur, called Centaurus, was the son of the god Apollo and water spirit Stilbe. He had a human twin brother, Lapithes.

🐎 Legend has it that Centaurus lived with the horses in the mountains above his brother's village, and had many centaur children.

🐎 Chiron was apparently a wise centaur who taught many Greek heroes including the warrior Achilles, the explorer Jason, and the super-strong Hercules.

🐎 Greek scholar Ptolemy Chennus, who lived 1,800 years ago, said that centaurs guarded Dionysus, the god of wine, during his childhood. Dionysus grew up to be a wild god!

🐎 Lucretius, a philosopher from 100 BCE, did not think centaurs were real. He said the horse part of the body would be fully grown after three years, while the human section would still be very small!

🐎 Since about the fourth century BCE, a constellation, or a pattern of stars, has been named after Centaurus, the first centaur.

Legend

At war with humans

Twin brothers Centaurus, a centaur, and Lapithes, who was human, did not like each other, and it was said that for many years centaurs and humans were at war.

In many myths, the centaurs are wild, dangerous creatures. One day, at a wedding feast, the centaurs were drunk and disrespectful, and a huge battle began. The Greek hero, Theseus, was there, and with his help the humans banished all the centaurs. It is said that this is why there are none left today.

75

Leviathan

- The leviathan is a sea monster mentioned in the Bible. It is said to be a wriggling serpent covered in huge armoured scales that are both hard and sharp.

- According to the Biblical Psalm 74, Leviathan had many heads. Other writers said its eyes shone as brightly as the rising sun.

- The word for "whale" in Hebrew (the language spoken in Israel) is "livyatn", the same as the terrible monster from Hebrew myths.

- The sea monster myth is much older than the Bible. As long as 8,000 years ago, the people of the city of Ugarit, in what is now Syria, believed in a sea god called Yammu, who kept a monstrous sea snake called Lotan.

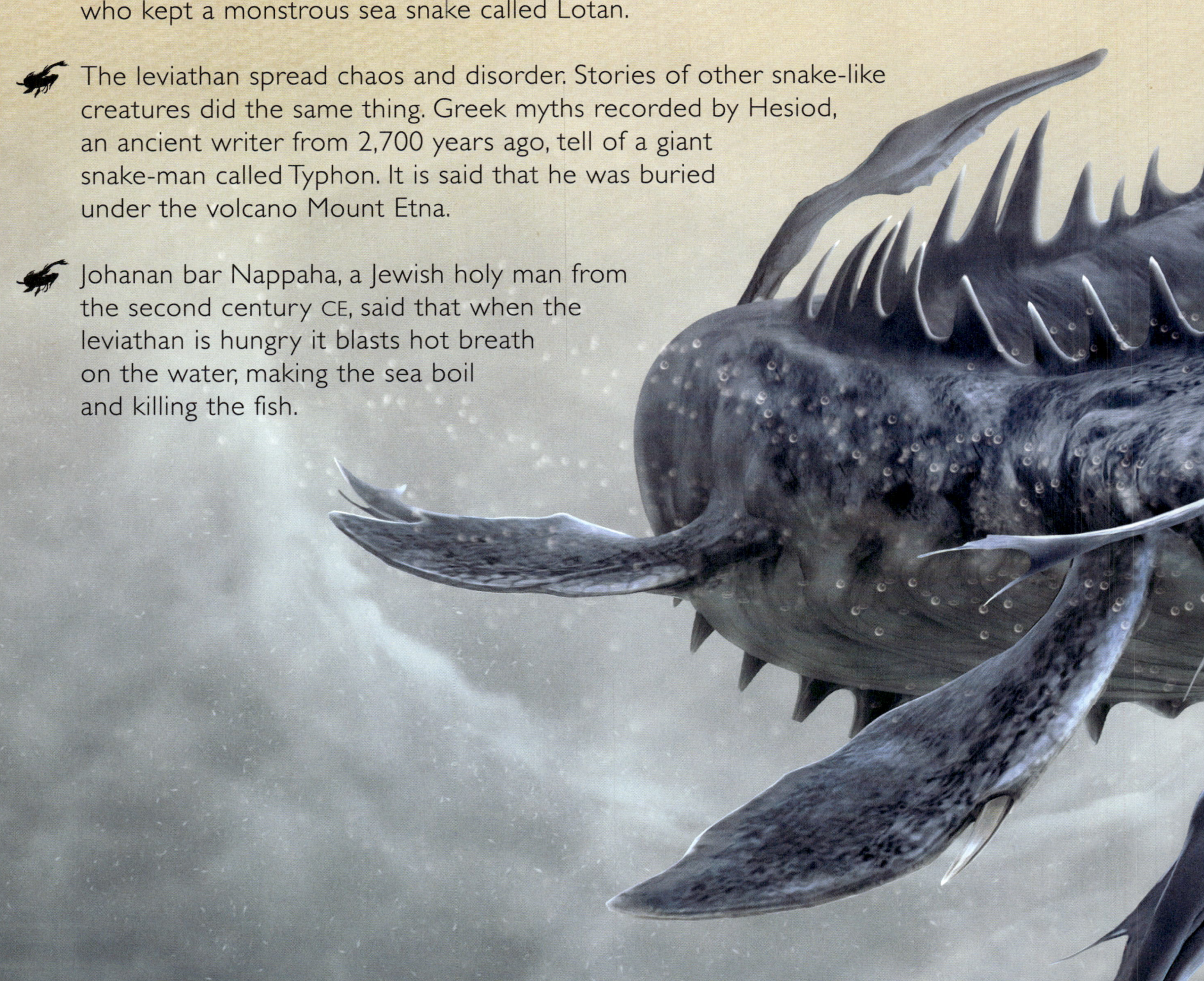

- The leviathan spread chaos and disorder. Stories of other snake-like creatures did the same thing. Greek myths recorded by Hesiod, an ancient writer from 2,700 years ago, tell of a giant snake-man called Typhon. It is said that he was buried under the volcano Mount Etna.

- Johanan bar Nappaha, a Jewish holy man from the second century CE, said that when the leviathan is hungry it blasts hot breath on the water, making the sea boil and killing the fish.

Ancient Egyptians also had a sea-snake god similar to the Leviathan called Apep. Apep was the ruler of darkness and chaos who, legend has it, always lies just out of sight beyond the horizon.

Legend

Killed by God

The story of the Leviathan was put together by several writers over many hundreds of years. Rashi, a Jewish rabbi from the eleventh century, wrote that God had originally created two Leviathans, but realized that if they bred they would eat the entire world. He decided to kill the female one. According the Biblical Psalm 74, God parted the sea and pulled up the monster. He then crushed its heads before dropping the pieces on the desert as food for the creatures that lived there.

77

Sphinx

- Pictures and statues of sphinxes appear in the temples and tombs of Egypt, and some are thought to show the faces of dead pharaohs.

- The largest is the Great Sphinx statue near the Pyramids in Giza, Egypt. It is 3,400 years old and is 73 m (240 ft) long—almost as long as a soccer pitch!

- Modern Egyptians called the Great Sphinx, the Terrifying One, or the Father of Dread.

- About 3,000 years ago, Greek writers such as Hesiod, included a demon called Sphinx in their stories, and it became a symbol of bad luck in ancient Greece.

Legend

Riddle of the Sphinx

The Greek playwright Sophocles wrote a play called *Oedipus Rex* in 429 BCE. In it Oedipus meets the Sphinx at the gates of Thebes. She asks him to solve a riddle—and says she will eat him if he does not get the answer right: "Which creature has one voice and yet becomes four-footed and two-footed and three-footed?" Oedipus solves the riddle: A human, because he crawls on all fours as a baby, then walks on two feet as an adult, and then uses a walking stick in old age. The Sphinx was so angry that Oedipus had got the answer right that she threw herself off a high mountain and died.

- While the Greek sphinx was a woman with a lion's body, in Egypt the sphinx usually had a man's head but it varied.

- Persian legends do not include the sphinx but do tell stories about another lion-man creature called the manticore—which means "man eater".

Fantasy world

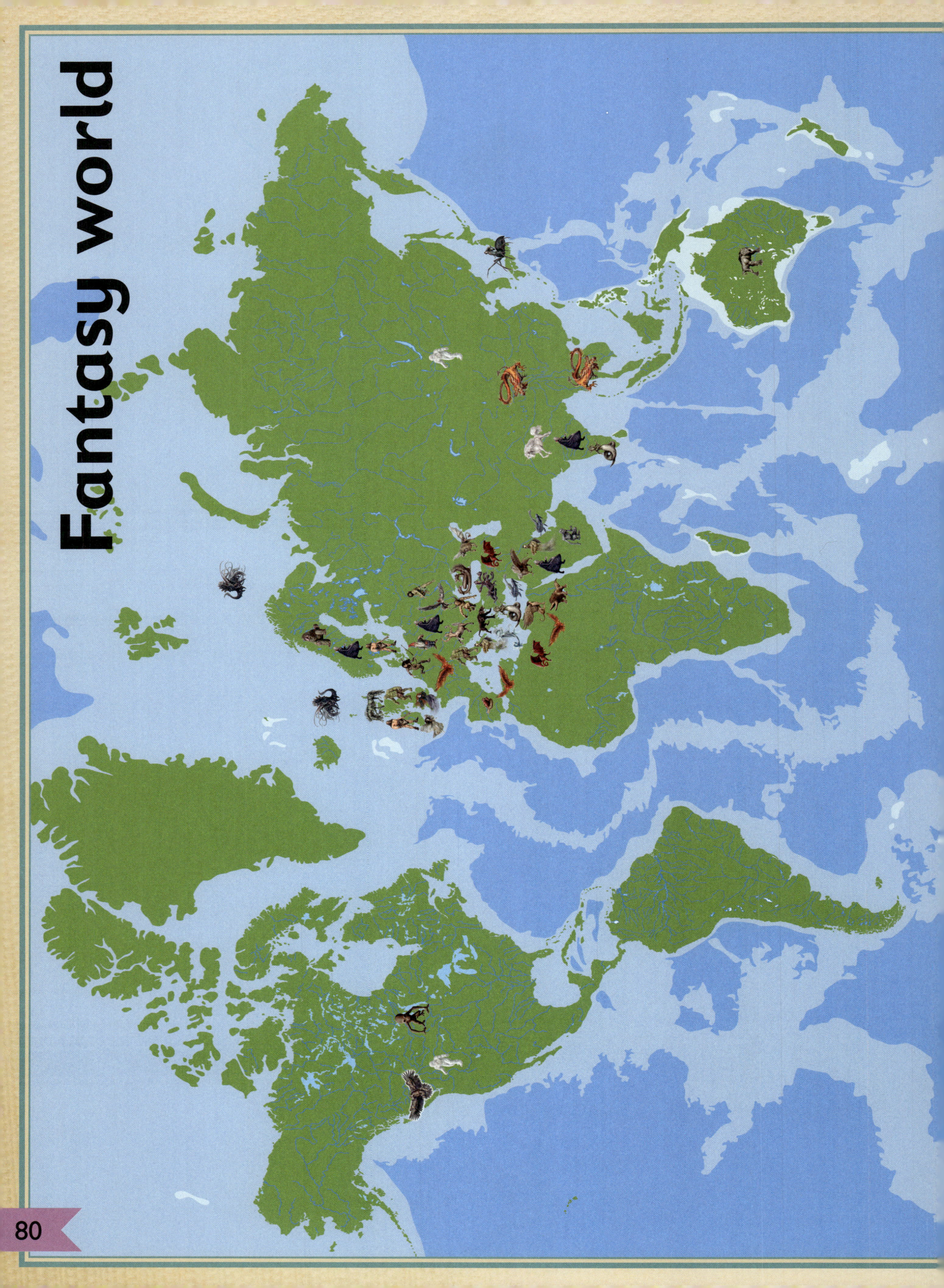